GHOST HAUNTINGS

AMERICA'S MOST HAUNTED PLACES

by Don Roff

SPOOKS, SPIRITS,

WHAT WAS THAT?

You're sitting alone in your living room one night. Suddenly, you feel a cold rush of air on your neck. Is it only a wintry draft? Then you feel as if someone is standing next to you—but no one is there. Is it merely your imagination? Or something else?

If it was supernatural, it can probably never be explained. Only you can say, with some wonder, if it was a normal occurrence or a paranormal one.

EXPLAINING THE UNEXPLAINED

The ghostly book you're now holding contains stories of the unexplained. It presents information based, in part, on accounts from people who witnessed the supernatural events firsthand. Some of the events might be true, and some are perhaps not—it will be ultimately up to you to decide.

! HOW TO USE THIS BOOK

This book comes with special slides and a "ghost viewer." Each of the slides corresponds to one of the ghostly stories in the book. Look for the silver-colored tab in the bottom right corner of the pages in this book to find out which slide goes with the story on that page. The spooky three-dimensional photograph will send chills down your spine and enhance your ghostly reading experience.

Technical ghost hunter words in bold are defined on the glossary on page 32.

GETTYSBURG BATTI

DURING THE CIVIL WAR, THE BATTLE AT GETTYSBURG, PENNSYLVANIA, WAS THE MOST MURDEROUS BATTLE EVER FOUGHT ON AMERICAN SOIL. ON JULY 1, 1863, CONFEDERATE GENERAL ROBERT E. LEE LED HIS TROOPS FROM NORTHERN VIRGINIA TO GETTYSBURG. UNION GENERAL GEORGE G. MEADE CHALLENGED LEE THERE AND A THREE-DAY BATTLE ERUPTED. THE BATTLE AT GETTYSBURG WAS ONE OF THE MOST VIOLENT AND BLOODY FIGHTS IN THE WAR, RESULTING IN 51,000 CASUALTIES. BECAUSE OF THE BRUTAL HAND-TO-HAND COMBAT AND HIGH NUMBER OF DEATHS, IT IS BELIEVED THAT NEARLY ALL 40 MILES OF THE GETTYSBURG BATTLEFIELD ARE STILL ACTIVE WITH PARANORMAL STIRRINGS.

THE DEVIL'S DEN

One of the most haunted locations in Gettysburg is a rocky area bursting with massive boulders and resembling a lion's den. It is called Devil's Den. Due to the unusual layout, a Confederate sharpshooter engaged in battle was able to hide behind the rocks and kill hundreds of soldiers as they passed. But Union soldiers finally caught on. Using a combination of field glasses and mirrors to determine the sharpshooter's location, they were able to kill the sniper.

During the Civil War, photography was new. Legend has it that photographer Alexander Gardner was at Devil's Den snapping pictures directly after the battle. In order to shoot more dramatic photos, he told his assistants to move the bodies of dead soldiers to different locations. It is believed that since these men were not left in their final resting places, their souls have never found peace.

From that day on, photographers have had trouble taking pictures in Devil's Den. People have tried to take photos, only to have their camera batteries suddenly die. Or there would be a strange haze over the photos, or nothing but a black frame. Could it be the Civil War soldiers' revenge for having been disturbed all those years ago?

FIELD

TODAY, GETTYSBURG IS A MAJOR TOURIST ATTRACTION. ON THE FORMER BATTLEGROUNDS, COSTUMED VOLUNTEERS REGULARLY REENACT THE BATTLES FOR THE ENJOYMENT OF VISITING TOURISTS. HOWEVER, THERE HAVE BEEN NUMEROUS REPORTS OF VISITORS WITNESSING A "REENACTMENT" ON A DAY WHEN ONE WAS NOT SCHEDULED AND NO ACTORS WERE EVEN IN THE AREA. DID THE TOURISTS SEE GHOSTS OF THE FALLEN SOLDIERS, FIGHTING LONG AFTER THEIR DEATHS?

Civil war reenactors at Gettysburg

THE BAREFOOT MAN

A ghost who wears no shoes? There have been several testimonies from witnesses who have reported seeing a barefoot, rugged-looking man with a floppy hat and ragged clothes on or near the rocks at Devil's Den. According to Civil War experts, the "Barefoot Man" matches the description of the unkempt, poorly dressed Texans who were at Gettysburg fighting for the Confederate Army in 1863.

! PULL OUT SLIDES 1 AND 2. INSERT EACH SLIDE SEPARATELY INTO YOUR 3-D GHOST VIEWER.

CAN YOU IMAGINE SPOTTING THE GHOST OF A SEA CAPTAIN WITH A LONG RED BEARD AND THE FACE OF SKELETON? THAT'S EXACTLY WHAT SOME PEOPLE IN THE TOWN OF NEWPORT ON THE OREGON COAST ARE SAID TO HAVE WITNESSED FOR MORE THAN 130 YEARS.

YAQUINA BAY LIGHTHOUSE, NEWPORT, OREGON

Captain Evan MacClure was the red-haired commander of the Moncton whaling ship in 1874. Unhappy with the way the captain ran the ship, the crew forced the captain off the vessel at gunpoint, sending him adrift on a dingy into the open sea. Adrift on the stirring, violent winter waters off the coast of Oregon, Captain Evan MacClure, who probably drowned when his tiny boat was overturned, was never seen or heard from again.

However, weeks after Captain MacClure's disappearance, local residents along the coastline reported seeing a wandering ghost with red hair and the face of a skeleton. One resident said that the phantom captain told her that he was "looking for a place to stay and someone to join him in death."

Years later, the whaling ship captain was reportedly seen again, this time haunting the abandoned Yaquina Bay Lighthouse. Apparently, he found his place to stay, as he was no longer spotted walking the coastline again.

To this day, visitors to the lighthouse report sightings of the ghost of Captain Evan MacClure, as well as a ghostly woman in white. Could the ghost of MacClure have finally found someone to join him in death?

PHANTOM FOOTSTEPS

Only a few years after the completion of the Yaquina Bay Lighthouse, a man hanged himself in the keeper's house. Later, a lighthouse keeper claimed that he heard phantom footsteps following him from the house to the tower, often on a daily basis.

HOUSES

ST. AUGUSTINE LIGHTHOUSE, FLORIDA

The St. Augustine Lighthouse, located near the rocky shores of Anastasia Island in Florida, was built in 1874. Despite its picturesque appearance, it has a checkered history of death and despair. For more than 100 years, ghost stories have lured visitors to the St. Augustine Lighthouse. Visitors to the St. Augustine Lighthouse have consistently claimed hearing a female crying "Help me!" inside the stately tower. Mysterious phantom lights both inside the tower and around the grounds of the lighthouse have also been reported.

THREE GHOSTLY APPARITIONS

This haunting is said to have begun when three girls died at the St. Augustine Lighthouse during its construction. Since the lighthouse is located near a hill, construction workers used railcars to haul supplies. The three girls were playing around the rails cars and climbed into one. Unfortunately, the railcar rolled out of control, thundered down the hill, and drowned the three children in the sea below.

! PULL OUT SLIDES 3 AND 4. INSERT EACH SLIDE SEPARATELY INTO YOUR 3-D GHOST VIEWER.

ALCATRAZ PRISON

ALCATRAZ PRISON, NICKNAMED "THE ROCK," WAS CONSIDERED INESCAPABLE. THAT'S BECAUSE THE PRISON, LOCATED ON A SMALL ISLAND IN THE SAN FRANCISCO BAY, IS SURROUNDED BY FREEZING WATER AND SWIFT SEA CURRENTS. AMERICA'S MOST FOUL CRIMINALS WERE SENT THERE. ALCATRAZ WAS ALSO KNOWN FOR ITS STRICT TREATMENT OF PRISONERS—AND MANY DIED WITHIN ITS WALLS. ALCATRAZ PRISON WAS CLOSED IN 1963 AND MADE INTO A NATIONAL PARK. SINCE THAT TIME, PARANORMAL ACTIVITY HAS BEEN REPORTED BY THE PARK RANGERS AND NIGHT WATCHMEN WHO WORK THERE AFTER THE DAILY VISITORS LEAVE THE ISLAND ON THE TOUR BOATS AND RETURN TO THE MAINLAND.

"THE HOLE"

A small, confined space with no light, Cell 14D was where inmates were sent for bad behavior. It was nicknamed "The Hole." When the prison was first opened, an eerie incident was reported. An inmate in Cell 14D screamed to the Alcatraz guards that a monster with glowing eyes was in the dark cell and was going to kill him. The next morning, the cell was opened, and the inmate had been strangled to death.

During the prisoner head count later that same morning, the guards counted one extra prisoner. The guards who counted claimed to have seen the murdered prisoner standing among the ranks of his living inmates, and then quickly disappearing.

AL CAPONE'S BANJO

Al Capone, a ruthless Chicago gang leader in the 1920s and 1930s, was arguably the most famous inmate of Alcatraz. During recess periods when prisoners were out in the yard, the guards would let Capone practice his banjo in the showers. To this day, park attendants still report hearing banjo playing coming from the showers area.

Al Capone's actual mug shot

! PULL OUT SLIDE 5. INSERT IT INTO YOUR 3-D GHOST VIEWER.

MOUNT MISERY ROAD IS LOCATED IN HUNTINGTON, LONG ISLAND. IN THE 1600S, THE AREA WAS A SMALL FARMING COMMUNITY AND THE ROAD WAS USED AS A TRADE ROUTE. THE EARLY SETTLERS NICKNAMED IT "MISERY" BECAUSE THE STEEP HILL AND ROCKY TERRAIN MADE IT DIFFICULT FOR WAGONS TO PASS OVER. BUT THAT'S N ALL. STRANGE THINGS KEPT HAPPENING HERE. CAN ROADS AND HIGHWAYS BE HAUNTED? IT SEEMS MOUNT MISERY ROAD IS.

GLOWING EYES

Settlers purchased the land from local Indians for the equivalent of $25. The Indians warned the settlers to stay away from this area. They claimed that there were evil sprits haunting the old hill. Also, there were reports of mysterious lights blazing in the sky and a "man-beast" with glowing eyes that lurked among the hills.

BURNING HOSPITALS

In 1840, a mental hospital was built on top of the mount near the road. Not long after the hospital was built, a mysterious fire engulfed the place, and it burned to th ground. Many patients were killed in the blaze. Nearly 15 years later, the hospital was rebuilt. It was said that the smell of the burning building and the screams of the victims could be heard a night during the construction of the new mental facility. In a strange coincidence, the new hospital burned down only a mere

GHOSTS ON THE ROAD

According to legend, a ghostly police officer patrols Mount Misery Road. In the 1970s, the officer was killed in the line of duty on Mount Misery. It's rumored that his ghost still pulls cars over to this day and then disappears.

Another ghostly legend stems from an event that happened under the Northern State overpass on Mount Misery Road. A woman was driving her car when she got a flat tire. When she stepped out to change it, she was hit and killed by a passing car. People have said that if you park your car there at night and shut off your lights, put your car in neutral, and wait, the ghostly woman will push your car up a small incline until you clear the overpass.

PULL OUT SLIDE 6. INSERT IT INTO YOUR 3-D GHOST VIEWER.

IN A CITY KNOWN FOR CREATING ILLUSIONS ON THE BIG SCREEN, IT COMES AS A BIG SURPRISE WHEN REAL GHOSTS NOT CREATED BY HOLLYWOOD SPECIAL EFFECTS TEAMS ARE SEEN WANDERING MOVIE STUDIOS AND THEATERS ALL ACROSS TINSEL TOWN...

HOLLYWOOD SIGN

Originally built in 1923 to advertise a housing development, the sign that reads HOLLYWOOD on Mount Lee is perhaps the most iconic landmark in the city. On September 16, 1932, a 24-year-old starlet named Peg Entwistle, who was frustrated with her life in Hollywood, climbed atop the 50-foot "H" and then leapt to her death. Tourists and hikers have reported seeing her ghost wandering in the area and close to her former home on Beachwood Drive.

UNIVERSAL STUDIOS

Lon Chaney, known as "The Man of a Thousand Faces" for his incredible makeup and acting skills, has been reported haunting Sound Stage 28. His most famous role was that of the phantom in Phantom of the Opera in 1925, one of the most popular films at that time. He died in 1930, and visitors and filmmakers at the studio have reported seeing the black-cloaked actor stalking the suspended catwalks of the enormous building.

The ghost of an electrician who fell to his death in 1925 has also reportedly been seen wandering around Sound Stage 28.

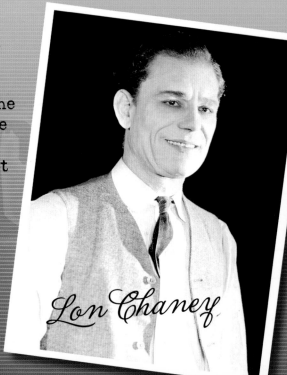

Lon Chaney

MANN'S CHINESE THEATER

Sid Grauman built Mann's Chinese Theater in 1927. Since the movie house was built, a ghost has been reported pulling the stage curtains and bothering visitors in the dressing rooms. The ghost of Victor Kilian, a famous film and TV actor who was murdered by an unknown killer in 1976, has been seen wandering the sidewalks in front of the theater, searching for the man who murdered him.

Mann's Chinese Theater

PARAMOUNT STUDIOS

Two well-known ghosts have been frequently reported at the famous sprawling Hollywood movie studio. The ghost of Rudolph Valentino, a celebrated silent movie actor in the 1920s, has been seen haunting the costume department.

At Studio 5, a ghost in ectoplasm form has been seen wandering the catwalks of the building. His phantom footsteps have also been heard. Some famous actors and staff have refused to work at the studio because of the ghostly disturbances.

! PULL OUT SLIDE 7. INSERT IT INTO YOUR 3-D GHOST VIEWER.

WITH LOOMING TURRETS AND GABLES, FRANKLIN CASTLE, ALSO KNOWN AS TIEDEMANN CASTLE, IS CONSIDERED THE MOST HAUNTED HOUSE IN OHIO. THOUGH THE MANSION HAS HISTORICAL IMPORTANCE, ITS POPULARITY IS DUE PRIMARILY TO ITS REPUTATION OF BEING A HAUNTED HOUSE. JUST AS IT HAS BEEN FOR A NUMBER OF YEARS IN ITS PAST, THE MYSTERIOUS FRANKLIN CASTLE REMAINS UNOCCUPIED TODAY. IS IT TRULY A HAUNTED HOUSE? THE NEXT TIME YOU'RE IN CLEVELAND, OHIO, DROP BY AND CHECK IT OUT FOR YOURSELF.

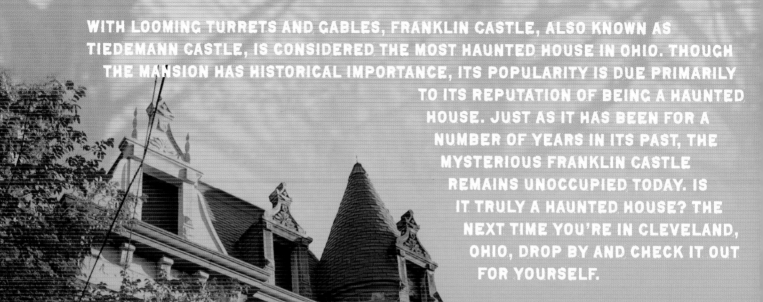

Franklin Castle

Tiedemann Family

THE HOUSE WAS BUILT IN 1864 BY HANNES AND LUISE TIEDEMANN. THE FAMILY LIVED THERE FOR 33 YEARS, AND A NUMBER OF FAMILY MEMBERS DIED WITHIN THE WALLS OF THE MANSION. THE LAST FAMILY MEMBER, HANNES TIEDEMAN, DIED IN THE HOUSE IN 1908.

LE

PSYCHIC DISTURBANCES

The Franklin Castle has had several occupants since the original owner passed away in the early 20th century. Some of the people who have lived there reported doors exploding off their hinges, chandeliers spinning around, lights turning on and off by themselves, vmirrors fogging up, phantom footsteps, as well as eerie apparitions.

Other strange phenomena include unexplainable crying of babies, gray mist moving in the halls, and the apparition of a woman in black peering out of the tiny window in the front tower room. When the Romano family moved into the dwelling in 1968, Mrs. Romano refused to let her children on the third and fourth floors because of the mysterious disturbances.

The Romano family soon hired paranormal investigators to investigate their haunted home. During the investigation, one of the team members fled in terror from the house. In 1974, the Romano family decided that the disturbances were too much for them to handle and left the house.

SKELETON IN THE CLOSET

Reportedly, the house has a number of secret passages that were added during and after the house was built. Once, a paranormal investigtor discovered a skeleton behind a panel in the tower room. The investigator immediately became ill after the gruesome discovery and lost more than 30 pounds in the following weeks.

! **PULL OUT SLIDE 8. INSERT IT INTO YOUR 3-D GHOST VIEWER.**

BACHELOR'S GROV

DO THE DEAD NOT STAY DEAD? SINCE 1989, NO ONE HAS BEEN BURIED AT BACHELOR'S GROVE CEMETERY, WHICH IS LOCATED OUTSIDE OF BUSTLING CHICAGO IN A SUBURB CALLED MIDLOTHIAN. HOWEVER, WELL-KNOWN PARANORMAL INVESTIGATORS HAVE REPORTED ACTIVITY FROM BEYOND THE GRAVE.

THE WHITE LADY

The cemetery received its name due to many single men being buried at the sight with grave markers dating back as early as 1830. However, one of the more famous ghosts is a woman known as the White Lady. She is seen frequently during the full moon, cradling an infant close to her bosom. She appears to walk aimlessly and is completely unaware of the people who claim to encounter her. There is no real evidence to say who this woman might be, but over the years, she has taken her place as one of the many spirits of this haunted burial ground. Other names for the White Lady include the Madonna of Bachelor's Grove and Mrs. Rogers.

GHOSTS WITH THE MOST

At the cemetery's lagoon, there have been a number of hauntings. A ghostly farmer with a horse and plow has been seen. Legend has it that in the 1870s, the frightened horse dragged the plow and farmer into the water, where they drowned. Now, their ghosts plow unturned fields among the tombstones.

In the 1920s, Chicago mobsters often dumped the bodies of their victims in the cemetery, lending to the already creepy reputation of Bachelor's Grove. Phantom cars have been seen driving around the roads near the cemetery and disappearing.

CEMETERY

CONTACT WITH GHOSTS

In December 1971, a woman claimed to have put her hand through a ghostly figure walking on the path just before the wandering anomaly disappeared.

Strange blue lights have been seen darting in the air, and one investigator in 1984 claims to have encountered a glowing yellow apparition of a man who appeared for several seconds, then dematerialized, bolting off in a flurry of red spots of light.

PHANTOM FARMHOUSE

During the 1950s, a ghostly farmhouse with a white picket fence appeared prominently several times both in the daytime and at night. No historical record of such a house exists in the area, but the descriptions of it are all similar. Witnesses claim the farmhouse has two stories, is painted white with wooden posts, and has a porch swing and a welcoming light that burns softly in the window. Popular legend states that should you enter this house—you would never come back out again.

! PULL OUT SLIDE 9 AND 10. INSERT EACH SLIDE SEPARATELY INTO YOUR 3-D GHOST VIEWER.

THE OLD SLAVE HO

ONE OF ILLINOIS' MOST HAUNTED SPOTS IS A HOUSE CALLED HICKORY HILL. IT STANDS ON A HIGH HILL, OVERLOOKING THE SALINE RIVER. BUILT IN 1842, THE NOTORIOUS THREE-STORY PLANTATION MANSION HAS ANOTHER NAME—THE OLD SLAVE HOUSE. THERE ARE CLAIMS THAT THE DEAD OF HICKORY HILL DO NOT REST IN PEACE. NOW OWNED BY THE STATE OF ILLINOIS, THE OLD SLAVE HOUSE IS A FREQUENT STOPPING PLACE FOR GHOST HUNTERS, PSYCHIC INVESTIGATORS, AND SUPERNATURAL ENTHUSIASTS.

A salt mine

THE SALT SLAVES

A man named John Hart Crenshaw, who owned a salt mine called Half Moon Lick, built Hickory Hill in the mid-1800s. In those days, valuable salt was often used as money to purchase goods and supplies. Workers were always needed for the salt mines and the work was backbreaking. Slavery became essential to the success of the salt mines.

THE TERRIBLE ATTIC

Crenshaw turned the third-floor attic of Hickory Hill into quarters for his slaves. The conditions were very brutal. The attic opened into a wide hallway and had a dozen cramped, cell-like rooms with barred windows and flat, wooden bunks. The slaves spent their time locked in their cells, chained to heavy metal rings. During the summers, the heat in the attic was unbearable. Many people suffered at the hands of Crenshaw. During the Civil War, when the salt mines began to quit producing salt, Crenshaw sold off his slaves and Hickory Hill. Crenshaw died on December 4, 1871, and was buried in Hickory Hill Cemetery.

NEW OWNERSHIP

In 1906, the Sisk family purchased Hickory Hill and invited tourists to their home. The tourists complained of odd noises in the attic, especially noises that sounded like cries, whimpers, and even the rattling of chains. Visitors to the slave quarters experienced sensations of intense fear, sadness, and being watched. They also reported cold chills, being touched by invisible hands, and feeling objects brush past them.

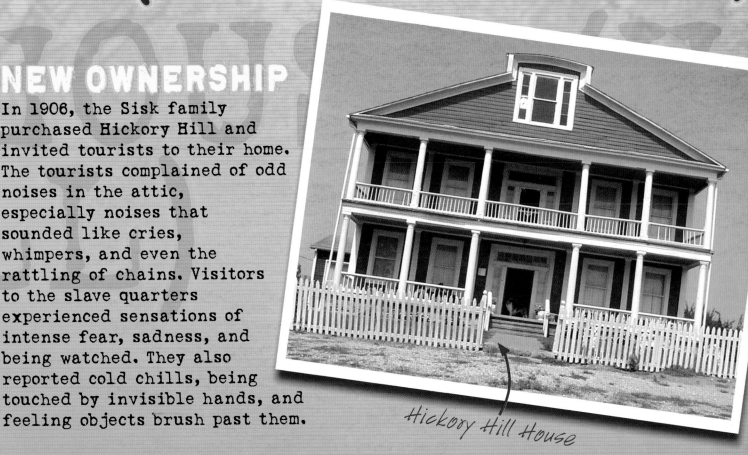

Hickory Hill House

John Hart Crenshaw and wife

GHOST HUNTERS AT HICKORY HILL

A ghost hunter named Hickman Whittington spent a few hours in the attic. Though he was in perfect health at the time, Whittington died a few hours after leaving Hickory Hill. Reportedly, hundreds of people tried to spend the night in the attic after Whittington's death but would leave, terrorized, before morning.

In 1978, a reporter named David Rodgers spent the night in the attic. Rodgers heard many sounds that he could not identify, and later, he discovered that his recorder picked up voices that he had not heard in the attic.

JOHN STONE'S INN

The actual Inn

ONE OF THE MOST HAUNTED PLACES IN MASSACHUSETTS IS KNOWN AS JOHN STONE'S INN IN THE TOWN OF ASHLAND. CONSTRUCTED IN 1832 BY CAPTAIN JOHN STONE, IT HAS A BROAD HISTORY—AND PLENTY OF PARANORMAL ACTIVITY—INCLUDING VISITS BY THE DEAD CAPTAIN HIMSELF.

CHEATING DEATH

In the 1800s, John Stone's Inn, then called the Railroad Boarding House, was said to be a huge hit among both travelers and locals. In 1845, an accident occurred in the building. Stone and a few other men were playing a game of cards for cash. A man beat Stone, but Stone believed that the man had cheated. A fight broke out, and Stone hit the man over the head, killing him. Stone and the other witnesses took the body into the basement and buried it. Legend has it that the spirit of the dead man, as well as those who swore never to tell of what occurred, still haunts the Inn.

A little girl is also believed to haunt the Inn. Her spirit is somehow attached to a dress that is stored in the attic. Many have claimed to see the little girl staring out of the upstairs windows. One female employee once took the dress home, and it caused so much ghostly chaos in her life that she quickly returned the dress.

THE GHOST HOST

Many hauntings that have occurred over the years at John Stone's Inn were said to be apparitions of the Captain himself. A distinct picture of him hangs over the fireplace in the establishment, and patrons claim to experience an eerie feeling of being watched when they are close to the photograph. Several employees in the building have claimed that they smell what appears to be cigar smoke, but that there is no one present who is smoking tobacco. They believe that this is the Captain himself, overseeing the guests and employees at the haunted inn.

! PULL OUT SLIDE II. INSERT IT INTO YOUR 3-D GHOST VIEWER.

FORD'S THEATER

LOCATED IN WASHINGTON, D.C., FORD'S THEATER WILL REMAIN INFAMOUS IN HISTORY. DURING THE PERFORMANCE OF A PLAY THE NIGHT OF APRIL 14, 1865, JOHN WILKES BOOTH ASSASSINATED PRESIDENT ABRAHAM LINCOLN, ONE OF THE MOST ADMIRED LEADERS IN AMERICAN HISTORY. SINCE THEN, THERE HAVE BEEN CLAIMS THAT THE FORD THEATER IS HAUNTED.

DEATH OF LINCOLN

John Wilkes Booth was a popular actor at the Ford Theater. On the night of April 14, Booth sneaked behind Lincoln and fatally shot the President in the back of the head at close range. Ten days before the tragic event, on April 4, Lincoln had a dream about his own death, writing about the dream in his journal.

PRESIDENTIAL GHOST

Since Lincoln's assassination, it is believed the theater is haunted. Along with other apparitions, the ghost of Abraham Lincoln has been seen, including reports of voices and laughter from areas where there are no people. Staff and visitors have heard the footsteps of John Wilkes Booth running to the presidential box, followed by the sound of a gunshot.

The ghost of Mrs. Lincoln has also been seen leaning over the balcony and pointing at Booth, saying that he has "killed the President." Apparitions also appear at center stage, lights turn on and off, and cold spots are often experienced in certain areas.

THE WHITE HOUSE

IN THE U.S. CAPITAL OF WASHINGTON, D.C., THE WHITE HOUSE HAS A REPUTATION FOR BEING ONE OF THE MOST HAUNTED HOMES IN AMERICA. MANY FAMOUS PRESIDENTS WHO HAVE LIVED IN THE HOUSE AND WORLD LEADERS WHO HAVE VISITED HAVE CLAIMED TO HAVE SEEN GHOSTS, PRIMARILY THAT OF PRESIDENT ABRAHAM LINCOLN. LINCOLN'S GHOST IS KNOWN TO WALK UP AND DOWN THE SECOND FLOOR HALLWAY, RAP AT DOORS, AND STAND BY CERTAIN WINDOWS WITH HIS HANDS CLASPED BEHIND HIS BACK.

CALLING ON GHOSTS

Several seances have been conducted in the White House over its history, but the majority occurred during the years of Abraham Lincoln. While living in the White House, he and his wife held many seances in an attempt to contact the spirit of their son, Willie, who died there.

Following the assassination of her husband, Mary Todd Lincoln sought contact with his spirit through seances and felt that she had succeeded.

Famous people including Winston Churchill, Harry Truman, Theodore Roosevelt, Herbert Hoover, Dwight Eisenhower, Jacqueline Kennedy, Ladybird Johnson, and Hillary Clinton claimed to have seen the ghost of Lincoln wandering around the Lincoln Bedroom or wandering the halls of the White House.

Mary Todd Lincoln

THE UNEXPLAINED EXPLAINED?

Now that you have experienced the unexplained in this ghostly book, what are your thoughts? Are the tales you have read simply stories made up to scare people or did something more happen? Is there truth in these supernatural events? It's up to you to decide, and perhaps, to do some of your own paranormal investigating. Have you got the guts to go ghost hunting?

! PULL OUT SLIDE 12. INSERT IT INTO YOUR 3-D GHOST VIEWER.

GHOSTLY GLOSSARY

ANOMALY – References any ghost that appears to have material substance, including a mist-like image.

APPARITION – a supernatural appearance of a person or thing, especially a ghost.

COLD SPOTS – Specific patches of cool air in and around haunted locations. They may be ghosts that cannot fully materialize.

ECTOPLASM – Often referred to as "ecto," this is the physical residue of psychic energy. Ectoplasm can be seen by the naked eye and is best viewed in dark settings, since it is translucent and glows.

PARANORMAL – Something that is beyond the simple human experience or scientific explanation.

PHENOMENA – Unusual events often associated with paranormal activity.

SÉANCE – A gathering of individuals in an effort to communicate with the dead, the spirit world.

Ghost Hauntings: America's Most Haunted Places

Written by Don Roff
Design by Ryan Hobson
© 2011 by Canopy Books, LLC
50 Carnation Ave., Floral Park, NY 11001

Image credits: (to come)

Every effort has been made to correctly attribute all the images reproduced in this book. We will be happy to correct any errors in future editions.

Made and Printed in
Guangzhou, China
May 2011
Tracking # 253944
ISBN9781607433392
Ages 7 & Up

10 9 8 7 6 5 4 3 2 1